Trotter Trivia:
The Only Fools &
Horses Quiz Book

Stuart Ball & Lisa Ball

Published by BlackCat Books

Cover designed with CreateSpace

First Published 2012

ISBN: 1478383399
ISBN-13: 978-1478383390

DEDICATION

In memory of John Sullivan, without whom…

CONTENTS

ACKNOWLEDGMENTS

The following books have been invaluable research tools in the writing of
Trotter Trivia:

The Complete A-Z of Only Fools and Horses by Richard Webber
The Only Fools and Horses Story by Steve Clark
Only Fools and Horses: The Bible of Peckham Vol. 1

We would also like to thank John Sullivan, Sir David Jason, Nicholas
Lyndhurst, Lennard Pearce, Buster Merryfield, John Challis, Roger Lloyd
Pack, Paul Barber, Tessa Peake-Jones, Gwyneth Strong, Kenneth
Macdonald, Patrick Murray, Sue Holderness, Ray Butt, Gareth Gwenlan
and everyone else who has been involved with Only Fools and Horses,
both on-screen and behind the scenes.

INTRODUCTION

Comedy shows have been a regular part of the viewing schedules ever since British television was still wearing short trousers. From the likes of Tony Hancock constantly rallying against the frustrations of life, right through to the lovable but accident prone Mrs. Brown and her boys, many memorable characters have strolled through the sitcom world and entered the hearts and minds of the nation.

Of the countless sitcoms that have come and gone over the years, one stands tall as the nation's absolute favourite – *Only Fools and Horses*. At the time of the screening of the very first episode, *Big Brother*, in September 1981, it was impossible to imagine that the show would go on to be the most popular British sitcom of all-time, garnering record ratings in the process.

When scriptwriter John Sullivan, fresh from his success with his first comedy series *Citizen Smith*, submitted scripts for a new show called *Readies*, it was met with much apathy by the powers that be at the BBC. With a change of title from the rather bland original to the more interesting *Only Fools and Horses*, the scripts were championed by experienced BBC producer Ray Butt. It was through his tireless campaigning on behalf of the show that the BBC finally relented and gave the go-ahead for production to start. Unfortunately, the BBC did not exactly go out of their way to publicize their new comedy and the first series played out to an average of eight million viewers, a fairly low figure in the days when there were only a threadbare three channels for people to choose from. Luckily, despite not really having a lot of faith in the show, the BBC persevered with it (something that seems to happen less and less these days) and, by the third series, ratings had risen dramatically. The rest is history…

Over thirty years since that debut episode, and nearly a decade since the last installment in the lives of the Trotter family was screened, *Only Fools and Horses* remains as popular as ever. This begs the question 'How has *Only Fools and Horses* managed to retain its place in the heart of the nation?' After all, many other sitcoms from that same era are now forgotten.

Only Fools and Horses had that rare combination of top-quality, very funny scripts featuring beautifully drawn and very real characters, combined with perfectly cast actors at the top of their game. David Jason and Nicholas Lyndhurst brought such warmth and humanity to the characters of Del and Rodney, that you felt they were part of your family or, even better, that you were a Trotter. Not since the days of *Steptoe and Son* had a comedy series managed to successfully combine laughter and pathos to such a degree. John Sullivan was every inch the equal of Ray Galton and Alan Simpson.

Pathos aside though, the most essential ingredient of any comedy series is, of course, laughter. *Only Fools and Horses* has provided the nation with many belly-laughs over the years. Who will ever forget the crashing chandelier or Del falling through the bar? How about the sight of Batman and Robin running through the Peckham night or the spectacle of an exploding coach?

All of these moments and more are included in this quiz book, which has been a true labour of love. It has been an absolute pleasure for us to relive so many classic moments in order to write these questions, which will hopefully leave even the most hardened *Only Fools and Horses* addicts deep in thought! There are 1000 questions in the book, which have been split into rounds of varying subjects. We sincerely hope you enjoy reading and playing along with Trotter Trivia as much as we have enjoyed writing it.

Until next time – Bonjour!

Stuart Ball and Lisa Ball

Nelson Mandela House
Peckham

Now appearing at The Nag's Head every Thursday.

TROTTER TRIVIA

Some fairly easy ones just to get you going!

1. What is the name of the block of flats where the Trotter family live?

2. In which pub would you often find Del and Rodney?

3. What 3 place names are mentioned on the side of the Trotter's faithful 3-wheeled van?

4. How many bedrooms are there in the Trotter flat?

5. What is the name of Del and Raquel's son?

6. Which of Del's friends works as a second-hand car dealer?

7. Which member of the Trotter clan was born in Tobacco Road?

8. Rodney is proud of his two GCE qualifications. In which subjects are they?

9. In which district of London do the Trotters live?

10. What is the registration number of the 3-wheeled van?

DEL BOY

Often voted the greatest television character of all-time, Del Trotter is the heart and soul of Only Fools and Horses. How much do you know about everyone's favourite fly-pitcher?

11. What Christian name is Del short for?

12. Who is Del's godfather?

13. Del once compared himself to which character from the TV show Dallas?

14. Del and his friend Jumbo Mills once opened a seafood stall outside The Nag's Head. What did they call it?

15. Which superhero did Del dress as in order to go to the Publicans' Fancy Dress Ball?

16. In the episode *The Second Time Around*, which one of Del's former flames reappears in his life?

17. When Del lay ill in hospital, what ailment did Uncle Albert suggest he may be suffering from?

18. What is the name of Del's father?

19. How old was Del when his father walked out on the family?

20. Del once sold paving stones to rioters during which famous riots?

JOHN SULLIVAN

The creator of Only Fools and Horses and many other classic British sitcoms.

21. In which year was John Sullivan born? 1942, 1944 or 1946?

22. True or False – John was born in Peckham?

23. Which classic novelist inspired John Sullivan to take an interest in English at school?

24. One of John's early jobs was stacking beer crates for which brewery?

25. John Sullivan got his writing break supplying sketches for which legendary comedy double act?

26. True or False – One of the episodes of John Sullivan's debut situation comedy series *Citizen Smith* was entitled *Only Fools and Horses*?

27. In which year did *Just Good Friends* debut on BBC1? 1983, 1984 or 1985?

28. John sang the theme tune to *Only Fools and Horses* but which Cockney music duo did he originally want to perform the song?

29. What was the title of John Sullivan's comedy series set in a hotel in Birmingham?

30. In the 2004 Britain's Best Sitcom poll conducted by the BBC, how many of John Sullivan's comedy series featured in the top 100?

BIG BROTHER

The historic first episode

31. Which character spoke the very first line in this, the very first episode of *Only Fools and Horses*?

32. According to Del, why is Trigger so called?

33. How much did Del pay Trigger for the 'old English vinyl' briefcases?

34. Grandad was upset because Rodney bought him a cheeseburger. What had he actually asked for?

35. Rodney and Grandad argue over how to pronounce the name of actor Sidney Poitier. Who does the actor they are watching actually turn out to be?

36. Who owns the stationary store that the briefcases were stolen from?

37. How many gas cookers did Del suggest the police had planted in his bedroom? 4, 5 or 6?

38. What was Grandad mistakenly trying to play on the Talking Chess game?

39. When Rodney left home, where did Grandad tell Del he had gone?

40. What did Del finally do with the briefcases?

DEBUTS

In which episodes did the following characters make their first appearances?

41. BOYCIE

42. UNCLE ALBERT

43. MIKE

44. CASSANDRA

45. RAQUEL

46. DENZIL

47. TRIGGER

48. MICKEY PEARCE

49. SLATER

50. MARLENE

51. JEVON

52. SID

53. ALAN PARRY

54. NERVOUS NERYS

55. JUNE SNELL

ONE-OFFS

In which episodes did the following characters make their only appearances?

56. THE DRISCOLL BROTHERS

57. RENEE TURPIN

58. TONY ANGELINO

59. JUMBO MILLS

60. ELSIE PARTRIDGE

61. BRONCO LANE

62. CORRINE

63. BRENDAN O'SHAUGHNESSY

64. OTTO THE DOORMAN

65. MR JAHAN

66. MIRANDA DAVENPORT

67. DR. BECKER

68. MR VAN KLEEFE

69. BIFFO

70. CLAYTON COOPER

TROTTER BY NUMBERS

This is a really tough round where the answer to each question is a number. Anyone who gets a full house here is a bona-fide Super-Fan!

71. In *To Hull and Back*, what is the combination for the briefcase that Del takes to Amsterdam?

72. What was the total amount of the Trotter family's shopping bill in *The Longest Night?*

73. When Del was posing as a foreign tourist in *A Royal Flush*, what number bus did Trigger recommend he catch in order to get to Park Lane?

74. How many children does Elsie Partridge have?

75. Uncle Albert is how many years younger than his dominoes-playing friend Knock Knock?

76. The lads on *The Jolly Boys' Outing* missed the last bus from Margate by how many minutes?

77. According to the Miami Police, Del's runaway jet ski ran out of petrol how many miles off the coast of Cuba?

78. In *Danger UXD*, how many boxes of tomatoes does Del put aside for Mike?

79. Approximately how many times has Del seen the film Wall Street?

80. When Rodney's ex-band appeared on Top of the Pops, what number were they in the pop charts?

GO WEST YOUNG MAN

Some questions about series one episode two.

81. What make of car did Boycie ask Del to look after for him?

82. How much did Del pay Boycie for the second-hand Cortina?

83. How much did Del eventually sell the Cortina for?

84. According to Del, the Cortina had only had one previous owner. What was his profession?

85. Which member of the Trotter family claimed to be 'one of the faces up West'?

86. What was the name of the cocktail that Del ordered in the gay club?

87. According to the waiter, what drink had Reg Varney enjoyed in Holiday on the Buses?

88. Who did Rodney buy a police uniform for, leading to the accusation that he was 'warped'?

89. According to Del, what was Rodney's nickname on the professional tennis circuit?

90. Who had Rodney supposedly beaten in the final of the Miami Open tennis tournament?

GUEST STARS

Can you match the guest star with the name of the episode they appeared in?

91. JOAN SIMS

92. PHILIP POPE

93. RICHARD BRANSON

94. CHRISTOPHER MALCOLM

95. TONY ANHOLT

96. BARRY GIBB

97. JACK HEDLEY

98. DANIEL PEACOCK

99. JONATHAN ROSS

100. ANGELA BRUCE

MIAMI TWICE   THE FROG'S LEGACY

IT'S ONLY ROCK AND ROLL   MIAMI TWICE

STAGE FRIGHT   HEROES AND VILLAINS

FRIDAY THE 14TH   IF THEY COULD SEE US NOW

A ROYAL FLUSH   TO HULL AND BACK

RODNEY

Are you a super-fan of Peckham's number one plonker?

101. What is Rodney's middle name?

102. Why did Rodney's mum choose this middle name?

103. In the episode *Healthy Competition*, with whom did Rodney enter into a business partnership?

104. Rodney briefly worked for Cassandra's father's printing firm as the Head of the Computer Section. What was the name of the firm?

105. How much was Rodney fined for riding a scooter without a crash helmet?

106. Who is the tutor of Rodney's art class at evening school?

107. What was the title of the book that Rodney wrote?

108. Who once said that Rodney had been 'blown out more times than a windsock'?

109. What is the name of Rodney's real father?

110. Who do Rodney and Cassandra name their daughter after?

CASH AND CURRY

How much do you know about episode three?

111. In this episode, the Trotters own another car apart from the three-wheeled van. What make is it?

112. What is the full name of the new business contact that Del meets at the Peckham and Camberwell Chamber of Trade Dinner Dance?

113. How many restaurants does the mysterious Mr. Ram claim to own?

114. Del christens Mr. Ram's bodyguard with the name of which James Bond villain?

115. Who does Del think Kuvera is?

116. Kuvera is actually the Hindu god of what?

117. How much is Mr. Ram willing to pay to get the statue of Kuvera back in his possession?

118. Does Mr. Ram belong to the high caste or the low caste?

119. Del informs Vimmal that Mr. Ram has offered to pay how much for the statue?

120. Can you name two of the four cities that Vimmal and Ram decide to target next?

THE SECOND TIME AROUND

On to the fourth episode now.

121. What type of snack does Rodney ask Del to get him from the pub?

122. What was the name of Pauline's first husband?

123. According to Del, who is the 'only living man to be treated for rigor mortis'?

124. What was the surname of Pauline's second husband?

125. According to Grandad, Del had been in more fights than which famous movie star?

126. Rodney suggests that Del and Pauline should announce their engagement in which publication?

127. In which seaside town does Auntie Rose live?

128. In which year did Auntie Rose first tell Grandad he could visit any time?

129. What high-flying profession did Pauline used to work in?

130. Before leaving the flat for good, Pauline left the phone connected to the Talking Clock in which country?

GRANDAD

How much do you know about the legendary Grandad Trotter?

131. What is Grandad's first name?

132. What is the name of Grandad's only child?

133. According to Grandad, his own grandfather had died fighting the Zulus at which battle?

134. Grandad once worked as a security officer at a warehouse near where?

135. True or False – Grandad once secretly dated Boycie's nan?

136. When Grandad worked as a decorator for the council, which mode of transport did he use to travel to work?

137. Grandad and his friend Nobby once tried to join which military outfit?

138. Grandad and his brother Albert once fought over which woman?

139. What was the name of Grandad's elder brother?

140. What was the title of the last episode that Grandad appeared in?

LITTLE BLACK BOOK

Both Del and Rodney have had a number of girlfriends over the years. For each of the girls below, can you guess whether they went out with Del or Rodney?

141. HEATHER

142. MIRANDA DAVENPORT

143. MONICA

144. TRUDY

145. SANDRA

146. IMOGEN

147. ELLY-MAY

148. BEVERLEY

149. DIERDRE

150. SHANGHAI LIL

151. BIG BRENDA

152. SIMONE

153. IRENE MACKAY

154. DEBBY

155. HELEN

DAVID JASON – TRUE OR FALSE

Simply answer true or false as to whether David Jason has made an appearance in the following television series.

156. PORRIDGE

157. THE GREEN GREEN GRASS

158. ROGER ROGER

159. OPEN ALL HOURS

160. LAST OF THE SUMMER WINE

161. CROSSROADS

162. CORONATION STREET

163. PORTERHOUSE BLUE

164. A BLOTT ON THE LANDSCAPE

165. DAD'S ARMY

166. DO NOT ADJUST YOUR SET

167. HARK AT BARKER

168. A BIT OF A DO

169. THE BILL

170. LUCKY FELLA

A SLOW BUS TO CHINGFORD

Okay, we're onto the fifth episode of series one now.

171. Which famous artist does Rodney claim to have had a conversation with?

172. Who claims to not be wearing a bra?

173. Which artist is a 'wally-brain' according to Del?

174. What does NSO stand for?

175. What does Del call his new security company?

176. Where is the bus garage that Del has agreed to keep secure situated?

177. When Grandad worked as a security officer, what was he falsely accused of stealing?

178. What name does Del give to his new bus tours scheme?

179. According to Del, where do 90% of all foreign tourists come from?

180. What is the name of Janice's Corgi?

UNCLE ALBERT

Some seaworthy teasers about Peckham's answer to Captain Birdseye.

181. Albert is the youngest of three boys. Can you name his two brothers?

182. What is the name of Albert's estranged wife?

183. The first time he saw his wife, Albert thought she looked like Ginger Rogers. Who did he say she looked like the last time he saw her?

184. What is Albert's favourite alcoholic tipple?

185. True or False – Albert served in both the Royal and Merchant Navy?

186. When Uncle Albert first appeared, what did he tell Rodney his nickname was?

187. While serving aboard HMS Peerless, Albert inadvertently sank the ship by running into which American aircraft carrier?

188. What is Albert's middle name?

189. Before Albert moved in with Del and Rodney, with whom had he been living?

190. After the Trotters became millionaires, who did Albert move to the coast with?

NICHOLAS LYNDHURST

How would you rate your knowledge of one of Britain's best and busiest comic actors?

191. In what year was Nicholas Lyndhurst born? 1959, 1961 or 1963?

192. True or False – Nicholas's first television work was for BBC Schools?

193. When he was just 17, Nicholas landed a part in which Ronnie Barker comedy series?

194. What was the name of his character in the Carla Lane sitcom *Butterflies*?

195. Who played Nicholas Lyndhurst's girlfriend in the ITV sitcom *The Two of Us*?

196. Which former Doctor Who was cast as Lyndhurst's grandfather in this series?

197. Nicholas played MI5 agent Peter Chapman in which comedy series?

198. Which writing duo created the popular comedy series *Goodnight Sweetheart*?

199. How many series of *Goodnight Sweetheart* were made? 3, 6 or 8?

200. In the *Only Fools and Horses* prequel, *Rock and Chips*, what part does Nicholas Lyndhurst play?

THE RUSSIANS ARE COMING

Some teasers concerning episode six.

201. According to Del, who has got 'a mind like a brown paper envelope'?

202. How many tons of lead does Del salvage from the demolition site?

203. What pre-fabricated structure does the lead turn out to be part of?

204. What is the name of the policeman who stops Del for speeding?

205. Finish this line from Del – "Mine is not to reason why…"

206. According to Grandad, what is the only war Del has ever fought?

207. What prevented Grandad's brother George from convincing the army he was only 14?

208. Which famous World War II battle did George end up fighting at?

209. Grandad thinks the quote 'war is hell' was said by Alan Ladd or which other actor?

210. Which actor does Rodney think provided the quote?

CHRISTMAS CRACKERS

The very first seasonal special.

211. *Christmas Crackers* was first broadcast on the 28th December of which year?

212. True or False – Both Boycie and Trigger appear in this episode?

213. Who bought Rodney a book on body language for Christmas?

214. Grandad cooked the turkey with what still inside it?

215. Who are Shirley, Shayne and Shaun's mum and dad?

216. What is Grandad's cooking forte?

217. What form of entertainment does Rodney profess to not liking?

218. Where do Del and Rodney go out to on Christmas night?

219. Which friend of Del's do they bump into there?

220. According to Del, Rodney has had more dogs than who?

GUEST STARS 2

Can you match the guest star with the name of the episode they appeared in?

221. ROSALIND KNIGHT

222. ROY MARSDEN

223. VAS BLACKWOOD

224. ROBERT GLENISTER

225. CHRISTOPHER RYAN

226. MICHAEL FENTON STEVENS

227. MICHAEL JAYSTON

228. PHIL CORNWELL

229. CAROL CLEVELAND

230. NICHOLAS COURTNEY

DATES   THE JOLLY BOYS' OUTING

LITTLE PROBLEMS   MODERN MEN

THE MIRACLE OF PECKHAM   THE LONGEST NIGHT

MOTHER NATURE'S SON   TIME ON OUR HANDS

LITTLE PROBLEMS   THE UNLUCKY WINNER IS

TRIGGER

The country's most famous road sweeper.

231. What is Trigger's real full name?

232. What name does Trigger always call Rodney by?

233. True or False – Trigger is an only child?

234. After having 3000 Green Shield stamps planted on him by Roy Slater, how many months did Trigger spend in a Young Offenders' Home?

235. Which film actress does Trigger confess he 'used to fancy'?

236. What is the name of Trigger's tomboy cousin?

237. Which councilor presented Trigger with a medal for services to the community?

238. Trigger's 'old broom' has had 17 new heads and how many new handles?

239. Mike once barred Trigger from The Nag's Head for stealing what?

240. What is the name of Trigger's niece, over whom Del and Rodney fight for affections?

THE LONG LEGS OF THE LAW

We are on to series 2 now. Where does time fly to?

241. As the episode opens, what is Grandad searching for?

242. Who did Monkey Harris team up with to put in false ceilings?

243. Which 'romantic' film did Rodney take Sandra to see?

244. According to Del, which record by The Police does Rodney own?

245. Which member of the Trotter family has 'had a lot of sobering thoughts' in his time?

246. As well as taking Sandra to the pictures, Rodney also bought her a doner kebab and a packet of what?

247. How long did Sandra give Rodney to clear the flat?

248. Where is there an all-night sandwich bar?

249. What does Rodney want to leave to medical science?

250. Rodney asks Del if he can keep a bottle of what?

ASHES TO ASHES

No, not the David Bowie song, These are questions on episode two of the second series.

251. According to Del, the authentic French tights he is selling are 'as worn by' whose mum?

252. What was the name of Trigger's nan?

253. Whose dad caught Rodney with his jeans on back to front?

254. According to the man himself, who died a couple of years before Trigger was born?

255. True or False – Trigger's grandad Arthur was also a road sweeper?

256. After feeling under pressure, Trigger is looking forward to the discos, nightclubs. golden beaches and blue skies of where?

257. How many years did Trigger's grandparents spend not talking to each other?

258. Where does Grandad first suggest Arthur's ashes are scattered?

259. Where do Del and Rodney attempt to perform a 'burial at sea'?

260. How many times was Trigger's nan married?

A LOSING STREAK

Let's continue with more questions on series two, shall we?

261. What unusual item did a Scottish comrade give to Grandad during the war?

262. How many bottles of their home-made perfume did Del and Rodney manage to sell?

263. How much did Del lose at the previous night's poker game?

264. At which race course did Grandad have a 25-1 winner?

265. How much money did Rodney manage to raise from returning the empties?

266. According to Grandad, Boycie knows more card tricks than who?

267. How much money does Del retrieve from the secret hiding place in the telephone?

268. What does Trigger give to Del to help him stay in the poker game with Boycie?

269. When Boycie reveals his final hand, it contains how many Kings?

270. Del's final hand contains two pairs of which card?

BOYCIE

From second-hand car dealer to gentleman farmer, Del's crafty mate Boycie has done it all.

271. In which high-class road is Boycie and Marlene's house situated?

272. What is Boycie's middle name?

273. Boycie owns a weekend cottage in which English county?

274. Boycie's brother-in-law is a painter and decorator who is known by what nickname?

275. What is the name of Boycie and Marlene's Great Dane?

276. What secretive society is Boycie a proud member of?

277. What piece of televisual equipment does Boycie buy from the Chief Inspector who lives next door?

278. True or false - Boycie and Marlene name their son Earl?

279. After falling foul of local gangsters the Driscoll Brothers, Boycie moves his family to a farm in which county?

280. What is the name of Boycie's farm manager?

NO GREATER LOVE

Some posers about the fourth episode of the second series.

281. As the episode opens, what item of clothing is Del trying to sell to Rodney?

282. Rodney falls for an older woman called Irene. What is her surname?

283. Which part of London is Irene originally from?

284. In which prison is Irene's estranged husband currently residing?

285. What is his name?

286. According to Del, Rodney falls in and out of love more times than which famous TV cop duo?

287. True or False – Irene has a son called Marcus?

288. After getting into a fight with Irene's husband, Del pretends his wounds are the result of falling down the stairs at whose house?

289. Who did Irene's husband mistake Del for?

290. What is the name of the girl that Rodney meets at the roller disco?

LENNARD PEARCE

Acquiring fame late in life, the earlier career of actor Lennard Pearce is not generally written about, so how will you fare with these questions about the man who brought the character of Grandad to life?

291. In which year was Lennard Pearce born? 1915, 1918 or 1922?

292. True or False – Lennard was once a member of the Royal Shakespeare Company?

293. While on tour in Berlin in the 1930s, Lennard met which infamous WWII figure?

294. True or False – In real life, Lennard was a heavy smoker?

295. In 1965, Lennard Pearce appeared in a stage play called *Busy Body*, which also included which other future *Only Fools and Horses* star in the cast?

296. Lennard once had a bit part in which long-running television soap opera?

297. In 1980, Lennard played a priest in *Witching Time*, an episode of a chilling television series produced by which famous British film studio?

298. True or False – The first choice to play the part of Grandad in *Only Fools and Horses* was Clive Dunn?

299. In how many episodes of *Only Fools and Horses* did Lennard appear? 18, 21 or 23?

300. In which year did Lennard Pearce sadly pass away?

HOOKY STREET

Can you match the following pieces of hooky merchandise with the episode that they featured in?

301. LOUVRE DOORS

302. RUSSIAN CAMCORDERS

303. CHRIS BOARDMAN CYCLING HELMETS

304. MUSICAL DOORBELLS

305. INFLATABLE DOLLS

306. MINK COAT FROM ETHIOPIA

307. PRE-BLESSED WINE

308. MENS' WIGS

309. LADIES' ELECTRIC RAZORS

310. INFRAMAX DEEP PENETRATION MASSAGERS

THE FROG'S LEGACY   AS ONE DOOR CLOSES

THREE MEN, A WOMAN & A BABY   HEROES & VILLAINS

CHANCE OF A LUNCHTIME   A LOSING STREAK

DATES   MIAMI TWICE   DANGER UXD

FATAL EXTRACTION

THE YELLOW PERIL

Okay, let's test you on the fifth episode of series two.

311. What is the name of the Chinese takeaway that Del has agreed to redecorate?

312. Who is the owner of this establishment?

313. How much is Del charging for the redecoration job?

314. What colour would the takeaway's owner prefer his walls painted?

315. Trigger reveals he stole the paint from a storage shed at which railway station?

316. Who was his accomplice?

317. What was the paint originally used for?

318. According to Rodney, his deep sea diver's watch tells the time in all the world's capital cities except where?

319. When the Chinese takeaway complains about the luminous walls in its kitchen, Del says it is new energy saving paint from which European city?

320. The cemetery is situated on the main flight path to which major airport?

IT NEVER RAINS

Straight on to the next episode of series two.

321. What is the name of the owner of the local travel agency?

322. How much does Del persuade him to knock off the price of a holiday?

323. Where do the Trotters decide to go on their holiday, which is 'away from the tourists'?

324. Which airport are they going to fly from?

325. What does Grandad put in the Spanish omelettes to compensate for only having three eggs left, one of which is 'on the turn'?

326. What is the name of the girl who mistakes Del for a Frenchman as he tries to chat her up?

327. Grandad reveals he was once deported from Spain and all its territories and dominions. In which year did this occur?

328. Where were the Trotter family living at this time?

329. Grandad and his friend Nobby became gun-runners during which war?

330. What offence was Grandad charged with at the end of the episode?

BUSTER MERRYFIELD

Just like Lennard Pearce, Buster Merryfield came late to the acting profession. Here are some teasers about the man behind the beard.

331. In which year was Buster Merryfield born? 1918, 1920 or 1924?

332. What was Buster's real first name?

333. True or False – Buster was a boxing champion whilst serving in the military during World War II?

334. In which profession did Buster spend most of his working life?

335. True or False – In real life, Buster was teetotal?

336. Whilst appearing in a small role in the 1983 PD James TV drama *Shroud for a Nightingale*, Buster met which *Only Fools and Horses* star?

337. In which year did Buster first appear in *Only Fools and Horses*?

338. In how many episodes of *Only Fools* did he appear in total? 30, 37 or 42?

339. What was the title of the very first feature-length *Only Fools and Horses* special to feature Uncle Albert?

340. In which year did Buster Merryfield sadly pass away?

DENZIL

If you want a parcel delivering anywhere, anytime, then Denzil is your man!

341. What is the name of Denzil's rather formidable wife?

342. How many brothers does Denzil have?

343. Which one of his brothers lives in Bethnal Green?

344. How old was Denzil when his family moved to London?

345. What is the name of Denzil's wife's canary?

346. What kind of cake did Denzil and his bride end up with at their wedding after Del offered to do the catering?

347. After being made redundant, how much money did Denzil receive?

348. What ailment was Denzil suffering from on *The Jolly Boys' Outing* to Margate?

349. Despite only owning a transit, Denzil set up his own haulage business. After taking advice from Del, what did he call it?

350. What did Denzil originally want to call his business?

A TOUCH OF GLASS

How much do you know about the first of the 'classic' episodes?

351. What song did the china cats that Del bought at auction play?

352. Grandad reveals that Del used to have a job delivering cigarettes around which part of London?

353. What is the name of Lord and Lady Ridgemere's butler?

354. Del thinks the painting on the wall of the Ridgemere's drawing room is by Van Gogh. Rodney corrects him by pointing out that it was actually painted by who?

355. Which famous university did Lord Ridgemere attend?

356. The chandeliers hanging in Ridgemere Hall are from which century?

357. How much is Lord Ridgemere originally quoted for having the chandeliers cleaned and repaired?

358. How much does Del quote for the job?

359. Rodney states that the Trotter name goes right back in history to which event?

360. According to Del, there are still four Trotter chandeliers hanging in which stately home?

DIAMONDS ARE FOR HEATHER

The Christmas special for series two in 1982.

361. What is the name of the singer performing at the Spanish Night in The Nag's Head?

362. What song does Del request he sing?

363. Whereabouts does Heather live?

364. What is the name of Heather's babysitter?

365. According to Del, what would Rodney most likely read at university?

366. True or False – Heather's husband is called Darren?

367. Who thinks that Del is acting like a 'born-again Ovaltinie'?

368. What type of rice does Del ask for at the Indian restaurant?

369. Who does Del buy the engagement ring from?

370. Heather tells Del that her estranged husband now has a job in a department store working as what?

JOHN CHALLIS

How much do you know about one of the most familiar faces on British television?

371. In which year was John Challis born? 1939, 1942 or 1945?

372. John made an early appearance in which classic Ronnie Barker comedy?

373. True or False – John appeared in an episode of John Sullivan's *Citizen Smith*?

374. In which city was John Challis born?

375. John has had two separate roles in which famous television soap opera?

376. In the *Doctor Who* story *The Seeds of Doom*, John starred opposite which Doctor?

377. True or False – John Challis has made appearances in the police dramas *Softly Softly*, *The Sweeney*, *Z Cars* and *The Bill*?

378. How many episodes of *Only Fools and Horses* did John appear in? 25, 33 or 42?

379. In 1985, John appeared in two episodes of which drama series set around a boat yard?

380. True or False – John Challis's house in Herefordshire was used to film the exterior shots of Boycie's home in *The Green Green Grass*?

HOMESICK

Here are some questions on the very first episode of series three.

381. What is the name of the Chairman of the Tenant's Association?

382. Who is in charge of Housing and Welfare at the Town Hall?

383. What does Grandad tell Rodney he has got for his dinner?

384. What is the name of the Trotter family doctor?

385. According to Del, the only fresh air Grandad gets is when he is listening to which radio show?

386. Del thinks that a choreographer is someone who works in which profession?

387. What television programme was Grandad about to switch over to when he collapsed?

388. What type of fruit does Rodney bring to Grandad's bedside?

389. Grandad gives Rodney an item that belonged to his grandfather. What is it?

390. In which war did Grandad's grandfather fight?

ROGER LLOYD PACK

How much do you know about one of Britain's busiest character actors?

391. In which year was Roger Lloyd Pack born? 1942, 1944 or 1946?

392. Roger's father was a character actor in his own right. Can you name him?

393. True or False – In real life, Roger has 'A' Levels in English, French and Latin?

394. Between 1993 and 1995, Roger starred in two series of which sitcom with a medical setting?

395. Also during the 1990s, Roger played the character of Jake Klinger in which popular BBC comedy series?

396. Can you name the character played by Roger Lloyd Pack in *The Vicar of Dibley*?

397. In which Harry Potter movie did Roger appear as Barty Crouch?

398. Can you name Roger's co-star in the sitcom *The Old Guys*?

399. In how many episodes of *Only Fools and Horses* has Roger Lloyd Pack appeared? 26, 32 or 39?

400. True or False – Roger Lloyd Pack was only the third choice to play the part of Trigger?

HEALTHY COMPETITION

Here are a few questions on series three episode two.

401. At the beginning of the episode, Del is trying to sell some toy dogs. Which Royal does Del claim has one of the dogs in his nursery?

402. Where were the toy dogs made?

403. Who does Rodney announce he is forming a partnership with?

404. What lot is Rodney originally interested in at the auction?

405. What number lot at the auction contains the broken lawn mower engines?

406. Who originally sold the lawn mower engines to Del?

407. Where does Rodney's business partner sneak off to on holiday?

408. How much does Del give to Towser in order to buy the lawn mower engines from Rodney?

409. How much does Towser actually give to Rodney?

410. Rodney believes Towser has a contact at which department of the GLC?

MIKE

The landlord of The Nag's Head was often taken in by Del's various schemes. How much do you know about Mike?

411. What is the name of the actor who played Mike?

412. What is Mike's surname?

413. How old was Mike when he first met his wife?

414. When his wife became pregnant, where was Mike working as a cocktail waiter?

415. Who did Mike once ban from singing in The Nag's Head?

416. Mike received severe burns to his scalp after purchasing a hair dryer from Del. What did the hair dryer actually turn out to be?

417. What is the name of Mike's old rival who now owns a nightclub in Margate?

418. What is the name of that nightclub?

419. Why was Mike eventually imprisoned?

420. Who took over the running of the pub while Mike was in prison?

FRIDAY THE 14TH

The third episode of series three.

421. Del arranges for the Trotters to go on a fishing trip to whose weekend cottage?

422. Which restaurant is willing to pay Del £10 for every salmon he brings back?

423. According to Rodney, who 'couldn't even poach an egg'?

424. Del, Rodney and Grandad pass the time by playing which board game?

425. What is the name of the Chief of Security at the Institution?

426. What is Grandad's definition of a 'psycho'?

427. What is the name of the local gamekeeper?

428. When a police helicopter passes above, who does Del say it is?

429. Del and the escaped lunatic play an invisible game of what?

430. How much per game does Del suggest they play for?

YESTERDAY NEVER COMES

Let's move straight on to the next episode of series three.

431. Which period does Del claim the cabinet belongs to?

432. How much does Del advertise the cabinet for in the local paper?

433. What is Miranda's surname?

434. Whereabouts is her antique shop situated?

435. The 'antique' cabinet was actually made during the reign of which monarch?

436. Which television programme does Del suggest Grandad go and watch on the portable television in his bedroom?

437. According to Rodney, most of Del's French phrases come straight out of where?

438. Miranda finds a copy of which magazine down the side of the sofa in the Trotter's flat?

439. What is the name of the auction house where Miranda tries to sell the painting that belonged to Del's grandmother?

440. The painting turns out to be a 19th-century work by which artist?

HOOKY STREET 2

Here are a few more examples of Del's dodgy merchandise. Can you match each piece with the episode it featured in?

441. KYLIE MINOGUE LP

442. JERSEY TOMATOES

443. ONE-LEGGED TURKEYS

444. ITALIAN SUN-HATS

445. SPRING WATER

446. TRIMMING COMBS

447. RAJAH COMPUTERS

448. VIDEO RECORDERS

449. 9 CARAT GOLD IDENTITY BRACELETS

450. SKI WEAR

FATAL EXTRACTION   THE JOLLY BOYS' OUTING

BIG BROTHER   DANGER UXD

HEROES AND VILLAINS   DANGER UXD

THE FROG'S LEGACY   MOTHER NATURE'S SON

IT NEVER RAINS   AS ONE DOOR CLOSES

MICKEY PEARCE

Rodney's rather untrustworthy mate is really a wannabe Del Boy.

451. Can you name the actor who plays Mickey Pearce?

452. In which year did we first see Mickey in *Only Fools and Horses*? 1981, 1982 or 1983?

453. Mickey once advised Rodney to have a two week trial separation from his girlfriend and then took her out himself to a disco at The Nag's Head. Can you name the girl?

454. When Mickey and Rodney went into business together, what was Mickey's official title in the business?

455. According to Rodney, when Mickey last went out with a girl he took her to a concert by which band?

456. Mickey decided to become a vegetarian after getting the sack from where?

457. Mickey also once had a Saturday morning job working on the photo counter at which high street store?

458. In *Little Problems*, Mickey started to sell mobile phones in partnership with who?

459. Mickey once sarcastically remarked that Rodney was being head-hunted by which *EastEnders* character?

460. How many episodes of *Only Fools and Horses* has Mickey Pearce appeared in? 12, 15 or 19?

MAY THE FORCE BE WITH YOU

Let's test your knowledge of the fifth episode of series three.

461. What rank in the Police Force is Roy Slater during this episode?

462. Who is rumoured to be selling pirate videos?

463. Who invites Slater back to the Trotter flat for a beer?

464. Which television programme does Grandad try to tune the microwave oven in to?

465. Can you finish this line from Del, talking about Slater? – "No, he ain't got a few grasses Rodney, he's got…"

466. According to Del, what could Slater be advertising in a few years' time?

467. What is the name of Slater's assistant?

468. How much does Del offer Slater to let himself, Rodney and Grandad go free?

469. As children, Del. Trigger and Slater used to pretend to be pirates. Which pirate did Trigger play?

470. Who pinched the microwave oven?

WANTED

Series three continues with this sixth installment.

471. Which local character does Rodney bump into on the way home from The Nag's Head?

472. To try to calm her down, Rodney tells her he is what?

473. Del teases Rodney by telling him that the police have nicknamed him what?

474. Who did Del once convince that they had the won the football pools, even though they hadn't entered?

475. Can you name any one of the three places in London that Del went searching for Rodney?

476. Where was the first place that Grandad searched for Rodney?

477. Which LP did Del play in order to wind Rodney up even further?

478. Which animal does Rodney try to imitate while hiding in the tank room?

479. Why didn't Rodney eat any of the canned food he had with him in the tank room?

480. Which local establishment went up in flames after a fight between mods and skinheads?

DURING THE WAR

He never talks about it but Uncle Albert was in the war you know!

481. Whereabouts was Albert when his lighter flame froze because of the cold?

482. Which one of Albert's former skippers used to wear a wig?

483. During his time in the Navy, Albert was a boxer. What nickname was given to his left hand?

484. Which one of Albert's crewmates died in Palermo Harbour after dropping a depth charge in nine feet of water?

485. Albert celebrated his 17th birthday aboard which ship?

486. What was Albert's main job in the Navy?

487. Whereabouts did Albert undergo basic parachute training?

488. Whilst picking up some prisoners of war from Hamburg in 1946, who did Albert ask to marry him?

489. What type of animal did Albert come across in Durban?

490. In *The Jolly Boys' Outing*, Albert discovers he inadvertently caused which character to spend most of the war in a prisoner of war camp?

CASSANDRA

How much do you know about the love of Rodney's life?

491. Can you name the actress who plays Cassandra?

492. What is Cassandra's maiden name?

493. What is Cassandra's middle name?

494. What are the names of Cassandra's parents?

495. Whereabouts do they live?

496. Which one of Cassandra's friends lives next door?

497. Where does Cassandra work?

498. Where do Cassandra and Rodney first meet?

499. Where do they enjoy their honeymoon?

500. How many episodes does Cassandra appear in? 11, 21 or 31?

WHO'S A PRETTY BOY?

This classic episode was the seventh installment of series three.

501. What is the surname of painter and decorator Brendan?

502. Brendan sold Del some paint which was supposed to be apple white. What colour did it turn out to be?

503. How does Del explain away the hump in the back of the coat he sold to the barmaid's father?

504. Before he heard the brewery were going to have The Nag's Head redecorated, which city was Brendan headed to?

505. According to Rodney, why did Grandad get sacked from his job as a decorator for the council?

506. How much does Del charge Denzil up front for decorating his living room?

507. According to Grandad, where does it state that 'everyone is entitled to a cup of tea'?

508. Using Corrine's phone, which old friend does Del call in Canada?

509. Who owns the pet shop where Grandad buys a canary?

510. How much does Grandad pay for the canary?

THICKER THAN WATER

The 1983 Christmas special saw the return of a long-lost relative.

511. What nickname has Rodney given to Del's latest girlfriend?

512. In which year did Reg Trotter walk out on Del and Rodney? 1962, 1965 or 1969?

513. According to Del, Reg once tried to scam a week off work with which ailment?

514. Reg has supposedly spent some time as a patient in which city's hospital?

515. What does he claim is wrong with him?

516. The results of the doctor's tests state that Rodney's blood group is 'A' whilst Del's is what?

517. Just before becoming pregnant with Rodney, Joan Trotter became friendly with a musician from the Locarno. What instrument did he play?

518. At the New Year's Eve party in The Nag's Head, Reg sang a couple of songs by which artist?

519. Where did Reg take Rodney on New Year's Day?

520. What job did Reg actually have at the hospital where he claimed he was a patient?

RAQUEL

A few questions about the girl who stole Del's heart.

521. Can you name the actress who plays Raquel?

522. What is Raquel's real full name?

523. What is the name of the dating agency through which Raquel and Del meet?

524. For their first date, Del takes Raquel to dinner at which hotel?

525. What profession is Raquel's father in?

526. Raquel once played a 'lizard person' in which sci-fi television series?

527. What is the name of the pop duo that Raquel formed when she was 17?

528. Raquel once landed the role of a flower seller in an American tour of which famous musical?

529. Whilst living in Margate, Raquel becomes the on-stage assistant to which magician?

530. What is Raquel and Del's special song?

MARLENE

Surely you know about Marlene? After all, all the lads remember her...

531. What is the name of the actress who plays Marlene?

532. What is Marlene's maiden name?

533. Uncle Albert takes a shine to Marlene's mum. What is her name?

534. True or False – Marlene's brother-in-law is a painter and decorator?

535. What kind of establishment was Marlene working in when she first met Boycie?

536. True or False – Marlene's father was a tattooist?

537. When Marlene and Boycie thought they were going to adopt German girl Anna's baby, what name were they going to call him?

538. In the episode *Video Nasty*, how many years of marriage were Marlene and Boycie celebrating?

539. What cosmetic procedure does Marlene undergo in *Sleepless in Peckham*?

540. In which series of *Only Fools and Horses* did Marlene first appear on screen? 2, 3 or 4?

HAPPY RETURNS

We're on to the first episode of the fourth series now.

541. Where does Rodney's girlfriend Debby work?

542. What is the name of June Snell's young son?

543. Who did Del describe as 'the greatest pal a bloke could have'?

544. According to Del, Grandad is in hospital with severe fraying of the what?

545. What is the name of the block of flats where June lives?

546. How many years has it been since Del and June broke up?

547. When Rodney pops round to June's flat to see Debby, he is carrying a bottle of brandy and an LP by which band?

548. Why is June's husband in prison?

549. How long has June been married to him? 5, 7 or 9 years?

550. True or False – Del is Debby's father?

STRAINED RELATIONS

The milestone episode which sees Grandad's funeral and the first appearance of Uncle Albert.

551. What relation is Albert to Grandad?

552. Who does Del ask to open up the flat after the funeral?

553. What was pinched from The Nag's Head the previous Thursday evening?

554. Who is Del's godfather?

555. What line of business does Del's cousin Stan work in?

556. The drinks for Grandad's funeral are provided by Mike. How much does the bill come to?

557. What meal does Del cook for himself and Rodney in the evening?

558. Which one of Del's cousins once sent Albert to Sainsbury's with a shopping list and then emigrated before he got back?

559. Where is the Seaman's Mission situated?

560. How much money does Del give to Albert?

SPECIALS

Christmas wasn't Christmas without a special seasonal helping of the Trotters. Here are a few questions about the various specials screened over the years.

561. At the beginning of *To Hull and Back,* which girlfriend is Rodney thinking of breaking up with?

562. Rodney becomes friendly with the daughter of which Duke in *A Royal Flush?*

563. What is the name of the Duke's racehorse?

564. Joan Trotter's old friend Renee Turpin returns in *The Frog's Legacy.* Whose aunt is she?

565. What is the name of Cassandra's boss in *The Jolly Boys' Outing?*

566. What is the name of the coach driver in this episode?

567. Who makes the sandwiches for *The Jolly Boys' Outing?*

568. To celebrate their new found wealth in *Mother Nature's Son,* the Trotters spend the weekend at The Grand Hotel in which seaside resort?

569. What is the name of Rodney's secretary in *Rodney Come Home?*

570. What kind of pet does Del buy Damien for Christmas in *Fatal Extraction?*

BIRTHS, WEDDINGS AND ANNIVERSARIES

There have been a number of special occasions in Only Fools and Horses over the years. How well do you remember them?

571. True or False – The midwife who delivered Damien was male?

572. As well as the Trotters and the Parrys, which couple attended Rodney and Cassandra's first anniversary dinner?

573. In which county did the wedding of Lisa and Andy take place?

574. Lisa is the niece of which Nag's Head regular?

575. How many pieces were in the dinner service that Del gave Lisa and Andy as a wedding present?

576. How much money did Del give to Rodney and Cassandra as a wedding present?

577. Who acted as godparents at Damien's christening?

578. Who took the photographs at the christening of Damien?

579. Which one of Cassandra's parents got drunk at the party after the christening?

580. What present did Rodney and Cassandra receive from Del for their first wedding anniversary?

HOLE IN ONE

Originally written with Grandad in mind, John Sullivan adapted this episode for Uncle Albert.

581. After going to the auction on his own, Rodney purchases a job lot of which product?

582. How much did Rodney spend on this purchase?

583. According to Del, the only thing they have sold in the last month was to Mike at The Nag's Head. What was it that Mike bought?

584. Who does Albert suggest should try becoming a toy boy?

585. If Del 'threw a fiver into the air', what would it come down as?

586. Who is the Trotter's solicitor?

587. How much are the brewery willing to settle out of court for after Albert's accident?

588. How many witnesses to the accident does Del offer to round up?

589. Before falling through the open doors of the pub cellar, Albert claims he was on his way to post an entry form for which television programme?

590. What has Albert been nicknamed by the insurance companies?

IT'S ONLY ROCK AND ROLL

Episode four, series four. Triffic, innit?

591. How many members are there in Rodney's pop band?

592. What instrument does Rodney play in the band?

593. Who is the band's lead singer?

594. Which famous 80s group are Rodney's band styling themselves on?

595. The previous Christmas, Rodney was trying to sell cricket bats which were supposedly autographed by which famous West Indies cricketer?

596. Who are the regular band at The Shamrock Club in Deptford?

597. Who is the proprietor of The Shamrock Club?

598. How much does Del charge The Shamrock for letting Rodney's band perform there?

599. After Rodney leaves the band, they perform on *Top of the Pops*. What do they now call themselves?

600. What is the name of their hit single?

SLATER

Test your knowledge of the universally loathed bent copper.

601. What is the name of the actor who plays Slater?

602. What is Slater's first name?

603. What is the name of Slater's mother?

604. For how long was Slater married to Raquel?

605. Where was Slater imprisoned after being caught smuggling diamonds?

606. According to Del, Slater collects informants the way other people collect what?

607. Who put itching powder in Slater's belly button at school?

608. Who put frogspawn is Slater's milk at school?

609. How old was Slater when he first joined the police force?

610. What does Slater claim his nickname is at the Met?

TROTTER MUSIC

A little musical interlude, Peckham style!

611. On one of their first dates, Rodney and Cassandra go to the Royal Albert Hall to see which rock legend?

612. Whilst pretending to be fourteen years old in Mallorca, Rodney meets a young fan of which boy band?

613. When Uncle Albert wins the talent contest at The Nag's Head, what song does he sing?

614. When Raquel asks for a 'little number by Bruce Oldfield' for Christmas, what does Del buy for her?

615. For her birthday, Rodney buys Cassandra an LP by which singer?

616. When Rodney's ex-band appears on *Top of the Pops*, which DJ introduces them?

617. Del sparks off a full-scale riot in Peckham by loudly singing which song late at night?

618. Which Beatles song does Mickey Pearce holler down Uncle Albert's ear on the coach down to Margate?

619. What is the first song Raquel and Tony perform at The Starlight Rooms?

620. According to Del, Raquel and Tony have just finished a sell-out season where?

SLEEPING DOGS LIE

A certain large canine makes his debut in the fifth episode of series four.

621. How much did Boycie pay for Duke?

622. How much per week does Del charge Boycie for looking after Duke?

623. Where are Boycie and Marlene going on holiday?

624. While chatting to a lady in the park, Del claims to be an expert dog breeder who has appeared in television adverts for which brand of dog food?

625. What is the name of the vet that Del and Rodney take Duke to?

626. Can you finish this line from Rodney? – "I've got a GCE in Maths and Art. I ain't got a GCE in…"

627. Who tries to do an impression of Duke over the phone?

628. Which famous literary character does Albert compare the hospital doctor to?

629. What did Albert say he had been given for dinner in the hospital?

630. What pills had Rodney been giving to Duke, mistakenly believing them to be vitamin tablets?

WATCHING THE GIRLS GO BY

Let's get straight on with the next episode in series four.

631. How much is Mike selling The Nag's Head party tickets for?

632. Who does Mickey Pearce suggest Rodney should bring to the party?

633. Rodney once went on a blind date with the Southern Areas Shot Put Champion. What was her name?

634. Can you finish this line from Del? – "Rodney, use your loaf, you're never gonna pull a tart dressed like…"

635. Who had Rodney bought his white outfit from?

636. Del claims that Rodney wears his heart where?

637. Albert's old flame Helga was missing the little finger on which hand?

638. What is the name of the girl that Rodney ends up taking to the party?

639. What does she do for a living?

640. How much does Del end up winning from Mickey Pearce?

AS ONE DOOR CLOSES

While we are on a roll, let's move on to the final episode of series four.

641. Which local painter and decorator gets the contract to fit out a new housing estate in Nunhead?

642. What kind of doors has the architect of the new estate decided to fit on all of the wardrobes?

643. What is the name of Del's mate who manages the local joinery works?

644. According to Del, when they asked for a loan, what did the 'bank that likes to say yes' actually say?

645. Rodney spots a possible money-making opportunity when he reads about a very rare butterfly that has been spotted in the local area. What kind of butterfly is it?

646. How much money is a local entomologist willing to pay for the butterfly?

647. True or False – One of these butterflies has recently been spotted in Hyde Park?

648. True or False – Albert reveals he can't swim?

649. How many wardrobe doors does Del end up with in his garage? 155, 165 or 175?

650. Which member of the Trotter family has a burial plot under a pile of stinging nettles?

SPECIALS 2

Another mixed bag of questions about some classic seasonal specials.

651. In *To Hull and Back*, what is the name of the ferry that the Trotters follow back to England?

652. In which seasonal special does Raquel make her second appearance?

653. Which Nag's Head regular receives a medal in *Heroes and Villains*?

654. Which auction house conducts the auction for the Harrison Watch in *Time on Our Hands*?

655. Which old flame does Del escort to the opera in *A Royal Flush*?

656. Del appears as a contestant on which television game show in *If They Could See Us Now*?

657. When Rodney tries to write a screenplay for a Hollywood blockbuster in *Sleepless in Peckham*, which movie star is slated for the lead role?

658. Who puts onion puree in Boycie's hair gel in the episode *Strangers on the Shore*?

659. What colour suit does Trigger wear for his blind date in the episode *Dates*?

660. What is the surname of the familiar-looking Mafia Don in *Miami Twice*?

DEL'S FOREIGN LINGO

Can you match Del's expertise in speaking foreign languages?

661. Which football team's name does Del shout out to locals when the Trotters arrive in Amsterdam?

662. Which German phrase does Del use to comfort Anna as she goes into labour?

663. What language does Del try to speak to the girl by the poolside in *It Never Rains*?

664. Complete this line from *Healthy Competition* – "No, not goodbye Margaret just …"

665. In which episode does Del believe his *'joie de vivre!'* will knock Raquel 'bandy'?

666. Del exclaims *'Vive la France!'* when the national anthem of which country is playing on his musical doorbell?

667. In *Miami Twice*, what does Del shout out when he realizes he is the spitting image of the local mafia godfather?

668. In which episode does Del say the following line? "There's a million quid's worth of gold out there – our gold. We can't just say bonjour to it!"

669. What does Del think Al – Qaeda is?

670. In which episode does Del try to impress Cassandra's boss with the phrase *'Fabrique Belgique'*?

FROM PRUSSIA WITH LOVE

This was the opening episode of series five.

671. In which year was this episode first broadcast? 1984, 1985 or 1986?

672. What nationality does Rodney initially hope the German girl Anna is?

673. Which Trotter claims he can speak German?

674. What does he actually say to Anna?

675. How long has language student Anna been in England?

676. Which two languages is she studying?

677. According to Del, recently he has had 'more relatives crawling out of the woodwork' than who?

678. What is the full name of the father of Anna's baby?

679. Which couple are hoping to adopt Anna's baby?

680. Where are the grandparents of Anna's baby originally from?

THE MIRACLE OF PECKHAM

It's straight on to the next episode in series five.

681. What is Albert eating for his breakfast at the start of the episode?

682. Who does Albert think Linda Evans is in the television programme *Dynasty*?

683. After trying to chat up a girl the night previously, Rodney is dismayed to find that her nickname locally is what?

684. What is the name of the trumpet player from whom Rodney steals his instrument?

685. After confession, how much does Del put into the Hospice Fund collection box?

686. How much more money is required before the Hospice Fund reaches its target?

687. What is the name of the hospice?

688. After witnessing the 'miracle' and realizing its money-earning potential, which Page 3 model does Del reckon he could get to open the new hospice?

689. When Del tells Rodney he has witnessed a miracle, what does Rodney say the miracle must have been?

690. Which American television network interviews Del outside the church?

THE NAG'S HEAD

How much do you know about the epicenter of the Peckham social scene?

691. What is the name of the very first barmaid we ever see in The Nag's Head? Nerys, Joycie or Maureen?

692. True or False – The site on which The Nag's Head is built was originally a burial pit for victims of the Great Plague?

693. How much money did the Driscoll Brothers give landlord Mike in order to buy everyone in the pub a drink?

694. Which medium one held séances in The Nag's Head function room?

695. How much did Mike charge for his Beef Bourguignon?

696. When Mike reveals his beer once won second prize in a breweries contest, who does Del say the winner must have been?

697. What kind of entertainment did Rodney have for his stag night in The Nag's Head?

698. Who won The Nag's Head Talent Contest?

699. What age was Trigger when he first went to The Nag's Head?

700. Sales of which food item fell after Albert started to sing whilst playing the piano?

THE LONGEST NIGHT

The third episode of series five. How well do you know it?

701. Which supermarket are the Trotters doing their shopping in at the start of the episode?

702. What is the name of the surly checkout girl?

703. How much money is the supermarket giving away as a prize to their millionth customer?

704. Who is the store's Head of Security?

705. What is the name of the manager of the supermarket?

706. What is the last name of Lennox, the would-be robber?

707. What time in the evening does the time-lock come into operation on the store safe?

708. Lennox claims that the police have given him a nickname. What is it?

709. According to Albert, he has known what come and go quicker than Lennox?

710. What is the closest Albert gets to a sudden movement, according to Rodney?

SPECIALS 3

Another selection of questions from random seasonal specials.

711. How old does Del claim Uncle Albert is when talking to Myles in *Mother Nature's Son*?

712. In *Heroes and Villains*, Del and Rodney dress as Batman and Robin to attend the Publicans' Fancy Dress Ball. What does Trigger go to the Ball dressed as?

713. Who does Trigger think Einstein was in *Mother Nature's Son*?

714. In *The Frog's Legacy*, Del gets Rodney a job in which profession?

715. What is the name of Abdul's cousin who checks the diamonds for authenticity in *To Hull and Back*?

716. In *Strangers on the Shore*, Del and Rodney drive Boycie to a business meeting in which European city?

717. Which airline do Del and Rodney use to fly to Miami in *Miami Twice*?

718. Which opera does Rodney take Lady Victoria to see in *A Royal Flush*?

719. Who gets 'blackballed' in the episode *Dates*?

720. Which Hollywood star does Rodney pretend to be in *If They Could See Us Now*?

TEA FOR THREE

Del literally takes to the skies in this classic episode.

721. Who does Uncle Albert reveal has been rushed into hospital at the start of the episode?

722. When Trigger's niece Lisa was young, Rodney claims she had more candlesticks than who?

723. As he only used to call her in an emergency, what nickname did Del have for Lisa's mum?

724. How old is Trigger's niece Lisa?

725. Which 60s pop star does Rodney jokingly compare Albert to?

726. What is the missing item from this list of food that Del buys for tea with Lisa? Chicken Italiano, fruit salad and…?

727. What is Rodney's sole contribution to the tea?

728. True or False - Rodney tries to impress Lisa by claiming he was a paratrooper?

729. Which birthday does Rodney claim Del will be celebrating soon?

730. Which two friends bring Del home from the hospital on the bus?

VIDEO NASTY

Series five episode five.

731. On Trigger's birth certificate, what is written under the heading Father's Name?

732. Who does Mickey Pearce reveal he is working for at the start of the episode?

733. Who is the head of Rodney's art group?

734. How much money has the art group been given to make a community film?

735. According to Boycie, what kind of watch does Mickey Mouse wear?

736. Who does Rodney choose to direct his film?

737. What is the name of Del's film idea?

738. Who tells Rodney that she once had a promising career in films?

739. What does Uncle Albert order from the Chinese takeaway?

740. Which two letters are missing on Rodney's typewriter?

WHO WANTS TO BE A MILLIONAIRE?

Series five comes to a close with a true classic.

741. How much does Del bet that Jumbo Mills is wearing a wig?

742. Jumbo has an apartment overlooking the harbour in which Australian city?

743. How much did the apartment cost to buy?

744. True or False – Jumbo owns a chain of fast-food restaurants?

745. Jumbo insists that his baldness is a temporary condition caused by what?

746. In which year did Jumbo emigrate to Australia?

747. How much money did Del give to Jumbo before he emigrated?

748. According to Del, what is the favourite champagne of Prince Charles?

749. What job is Rodney due to be allocated at Jumbo and Del's car dealership in Australia?

750. According to Uncle Albert, what is the only way to tell the difference between men and women in Australia?

SPECIALS 4

Another ten questions taken from various special episodes.

751. How many diamonds are the Trotters asked to smuggle back to England in *To Hull and Back*?

752. Which special is the most-watched episode in *Only Fools* history?

753. In *Mother Nature's Son*, who reveals he was in detention in the school science lab at the time that Del blew it up?

754. In the same episode, who advises Del to advertise Peckham Spring on local radio?

755. Who boils his vests and pants in a big pot on the cooker in *Fatal Extraction*?

756. What is the name of the bed and breakfast in Margate where the Trotters spend the night in *The Jolly Boys' Outing*?

757. What is the name of the owner of this bed and breakfast?

758. In *Strangers on the Shore*, who does Del buy a consignment of Slovakian log-effect gas fires from?

759. In the episode *Sleepless in Peckham*, how much money are Del and Rodney each left in Uncle Albert's will?

760. What is the name of the Duke of Maylebury's butler in *A Royal Flush*?

YUPPY LOVE

*Not only the first episode of series six but also the very first regular episode with the
extended running time of 50 minutes.*

761. In which year was this episode first broadcast? 1988, 1989 or 1990?

762. According to Albert, how long has it been since Rodney enrolled on
his 3-month computer diploma course?

763. Which character from the film Wall Street is Del trying to model
himself on?

764. Who was 'as useful as a pair of sunglasses on a bloke with one ear'
according to Del?

765. How many paper rounds did Del have when he was younger?

766. When he was aged 11, Rodney spent an entire Sunday trying to sell
DIY gas conversion kits on which all-electric housing estate?

767. Who thinks that Del's green trench coat makes him look like 'the
Incredible Hulk's little boy'?

768. Where is the Down by the Riverside club located?

769. How much does Rodney bet Mickey and Jevon that he can get
Cassandra to dance with him?

770. Where does Del reveal he was working when he fell in love with a girl
from Texas?

DANGER UXD

Another classic episode from the sixth series.

771. Where was Del's new video recorder manufactured?

772. What is the new name for Ron's Cash and Carry?

773. What is the full name of the owner of this business?

774. How many video recorders were in the consignment that Del purchased?

775. What does Mike offer to Rodney to help wipe the tomato stains off his suit?

776. Whereabouts is the plastics factory that Denzil recently won a contract with situated?

777. How many life-size inflatable dolls do Del and Rodney end up with?

778. Who owns the 'personal shop' in Walworth Road?

779. According to Mike, who currently has a 'face like a constipated rat?'

780. Which explosive gas are the inflatable dolls filled with?

SPECIALS 5

Yet more questions regarding various classic seasonal specials. We're spoiling you, aren't we?

781. During the game of Trivial Pursuit in *The Jolly Boys' Outing*, what is Del's answer to the question 'What is a female swan called'?

782. Which haulage company was Denzil working for when he drove *To Hull and Back*?

783. Which ticket tout did Del score some opera tickets from in *A Royal Flush*?

784. In *Miami Twice*, which seaside resort hosted the seminar which prevented Cassandra from going to Miami?

785. When Rodney telephoned to apply for his own job in *Modern Men*, which assumed name did Del take?

786. Who did Del purchase his answering machine from in *Heroes and Villains*?

787. After Rodney's disastrous date with Nerys in *Dates*, how much did the repair bill for the van total?

788. In *The Frog's Legacy*, in which year did Renee Turpin reveal she had moved away from Peckham? 1955, 1965 or 1975?

789. In the same episode, which explosives expert had partnered Freddy the Frog in his robbery of a post office in Plumstead?

790. Who was the very last person to telephone the Trotters at their flat at the end of *Time on Our Hands*?

AROUND PECKHAM

There's much more to life in Peckham than just The Nag's Head, you know. Let's take a look.

791. In which road is the Hari Krishna temple situated?

792. Who is the receptionist at the Peckham Exhaust Centre?

793. What is the name of the doorman at the One Eleven Club?

794. In the episode *Dates*, which local pub did Rodney reveal had a stripper on that evening?

795. Where is Alex Travel situated?

796. True or False – The Star of Bengal is one of Del's favourite Indian restaurants?

797. Where does Uncle Albert often play dominos?

798. Nelson Mandela House is just one of the tower blocks on which estate?

799. What is the name of the local newspaper?

800. Which restaurant is situated in Wilmot Road? The Golden Lotus or The Light of Nepal?

CHAIN GANG

Let's test your knowledge of the third episode of series six.

801. In which local establishment do we first meet retired jeweller Arnie?

802. According to Del, who 'talks with a squint and walks with a stutter'?

803. What is the name of Arnie's wife?

804. True or False – Arnie's two sons are called Glen and Stephen?

805. How many 18ct gold chains does Arnie have for sale?

806. Del puts together a consortium to buy the chains. How much money does the consortium have to raise?

807. Who is missing from this list of consortium members? Del, Rodney, Trigger, Albert, Boycie and...?

808. Who puts the most money into the consortium?

809. Who put £189.26 into the consortium? Albert, Trigger or Rodney?

810. At which hospital did Rodney and Albert lose the ambulance containing Arnie and the chains?

THE UNLUCKY WINNER IS

Let's move straight to the next episode in series six.

811. What is the title of Rodney's painting, which he completed when he was fourteen and a half years-old?

812. Which world-famous monument was the original subject of the painting?

813. Which model was Del on the verge of winning a night out with, according to Rodney?

814. Who does Albert have a date with?

815. Which brand of cereal hosts the competition which Rodney's painting scoops first prize in?

816. The competition prize is a week's holiday on which Balearic island?

817. As he has to pretend to be 14, which children's gang is Rodney 'conscripted' into?

818. In which position did Rodney finish in the skateboard derby?

819. What is the name of the male courier who meets the Trotters at the airport?

820. How much do Del and Rodney think they have won on the Spanish Lottery?

SPECIALS 6

Another dip into some classic seasonal specials.

821. In *If They Could See Us Now,* who telephoned Rodney claiming he was a representative of the Sultan of Brunei?

822. In *Sleepless in Peckham,* who was falsely rumoured to have run away with Marlene?

823. What is the name of the chain of health food stores owned by Myles in *Mother Nature's Son?*

824. In *Rodney Come Home,* Rodney attempted to make Cassandra jealous by taking another girl to see which film?

825. During their overnight stay in Margate during *The Jolly Boys' Outing,* Del compared having to spend the night with Rodney and Albert to spending a long weekend with who?

826. How many hairs did Denzil find in his porridge whilst eating at Sid's Café in *Fatal Extraction?* 2, 3 or 4?

827. In the same episode, who revealed he has pet names for his teeth?

828. Why is Frederick Robdal nicknamed Freddy the Frog in *The Frog's Legacy?*

829. While in Miami in *Miami Twice,* which country did many locals mistakenly believe Del and Rodney were from?

830. How much did the Marine Timekeeper watch sell for in *Time on Our Hands?*

MOTOR MADNESS

In this very tough round, can you match the vehicles below (complete with number plates) with the episodes they were featured in? If a vehicle has appeared in more than one episode then the answer you are looking for will be the very first episode it is seen in.

831. FORD CORTINA MARK II   OXL 825E

832. E-TYPE JAGUAR   UYP 694M

833. VAUXHALL VELOX MARK III   DJH 921B

834. FORD CAPRI GHIA   UYD 177R

835. LEYLAND BUS   KCH 106

836. FORD CORTINA MARK IV   OLO 77W

837. JAGUAR XJ6   TJT 705

838. ROLLS ROYCE PHANTOM 6   130 SKN

839. JAGUAR XK8   A3 TWR

840. COUNCIL ROADSWEEPER   ULR 981X

GO WEST YOUNG MAN   ASHES TO ASHES

TIME ON OUR HANDS   CASH AND CURRY

GO WEST YOUNG MAN   SLOW BUS TO CHINGFORD

HE AIN'T HEAVY HE'S MY UNCLE   CHAIN GANG

THE FROG'S LEGACY   CASH AND CURRY

SICKNESS AND WEALTH

This was the fifth episode of series six.

841. How much did Albert pay for his spin dryer?

842. How much did Del sell the same spin dryer for the previous week?

843. What does PMA stand for, according to Del?

844. Which room in the Trotter's flat does Elsie Partridge believe is haunted?

845. In which decade did people travel from miles around to consult Elsie Partridge as a medium?

846. Which animal shelter did Elsie used to donate all her earnings to?

847. How much did Del say he was going to charge people if they wanted Elsie to contact Elvis Presley?

848. What is the name of the GP who has taken over from Dr. Meadows?

849. Which city in India is she from?

850. What condition is Del finally diagnosed with?

LITTLE PROBLEMS

Rodney and Cassandra tie the knot in the final episode of series six.

851. Rodney and Cassandra have found a flat to buy but how much is the total deposit they have to put down on it?

852. How many mobile phones does Del buy from Mickey and Jevon?

853. How much does Del initially try to sell one of the mobile phones to Mike for?

854. After programming in the wrong data during his computer diploma exam, where was Rodney's unmanned space probe due to land?

855. How much money did Del give to Rodney's course tutor to make sure he passed the exam?

856. According to Boycie, one of the Driscoll brothers looks like he has been evicted from where?

857. How much money do the Driscoll Brothers claim Del owes them?

858. Who reveals that he had a learner sign glued to his underpants on his stag night?

859. Where does Alan say Del is taking him on the Wednesday after the wedding?

860. True or False – Boycie and Marlene's Great Dane Duke is at the wedding reception?

SPECIALS 7

Another selection of seasonal special teasers for you to have a ponder over.

861. Taken from *Mother Nature's Son*, what do the initials SWANS stand for?

862. Who was seasick on the journey to Amsterdam in *To Hull and Back*?

863. Which coach firm supplied the coach for *The Jolly Boys' Outing*?

864. In *Rodney Come Home*, who advised Rodney he needed to make Cassandra jealous in order for his marriage to work?

865. In *Fatal Extraction*, Del was selling ski wear made in which country?

866. Whose birthday was being celebrated in the episode *Dates*?

867. Which mafia gang member lent Rodney some of his clothes in *Miami Twice*?

868. In *Dates*, what kind of fish does Boycie threaten to add to his aquarium to stop Duke the dog jumping in there?

869. What did Uncle Albert mistake Cassandra's specimen for in *Heroes and Villains*?

870. In *Modern Men*, Rodney compared Albert's beard to which forest?

THE SKY'S THE LIMIT

How much do you know about the opening episode of series seven?

871. Can you name either of the two newspapers that Uncle Albert gives to Del along with his morning cup of tea?

872. Del compares Albert's laugh to someone trying to push-start what?

873. How old was Albert's father when he passed away?

874. What does Albert say is wrong with Rodney when he telephones Rodney's work to say he won't be in?

875. How much money does Boycie owe Bronco for decorating his vestibule?

876. What is the name of Bronco's daughter?

877. What was the name of the female high-flyer at the Council depot who Trigger describes as having a 'funny eye'?

878. Who calls Del to complain about a mobile phone he has been sold?

879. What is the most money Boycie is willing to pay to get his satellite receiver back?

880. At the time this episode is set, how many months have Rodney and Cassandra been married?

CHANCE OF A LUNCHTIME

Let's move straight on with the next episode in series seven.

881. Which play by Shakespeare is Raquel reading at the start of this episode?

882. Which opera does Raquel reveal she auditioned for while in America?

883. How many different national anthems does Del's new musical doorbell play?

884. How much does Del charge Trigger for one of the doorbells, including batteries and fitting?

885. According to Del, he misses Rodney like George Michael misses who?

886. According to Boycie, how will Marlene know it is him when he arrives home?

887. Which country has Cassandra recently returned from with her mum?

888. Who was the first woman in Peckham to smoke menthol cigarettes?

889. What is the name of the set designer that Del meets in a bar?

890. What does Del answer when he is asked what he thinks of Hamlet?

BEHIND THE SCENES

How familiar are you with the many great people who have worked behind the scenes on Only Fools and Horses?

891. What is the name of the comedian who acted as the audience warm-up man during the studio recordings of the latter episodes?

892. True or False – Ray Butt, the producer of the first five series also directed some episodes including *To Hull and Back*?

893. True or False – John Sullivan was originally against the idea of casting David Jason as Del Boy?

894. Who directed the very first series?

895. Who sang the closing theme to *The Jolly Boys' Outing*?

896. Which former star of *Hi-de-Hi* acted as the audience warm-up man for the earlier episodes?

897. Who took over as producer from Ray Butt from series six onwards?

898. True or False – John Sullivan is listed as Executive Producer on some episodes?

899. Can you name either of the two women who have directed episodes?

900. True or False – David Jason directed one episode.

SPECIALS 8

Another selection of questions on some classic special episodes.

901. What did Del purchase from Ugandan Morris in *Heroes and Villains*?

902. How much could you buy a bottle of Peckham Spring for in *Mother Nature's Son*?

903. Can you finish this list of ingredients that Albert puts in his pipe in *The Frog's Legacy*? Dutch tobacco, Navy shag and a...?

904. Who put on a 'dab of Blue Stratos' to go on the pull in *To Hull and Back*?

905. Who became a member of the Masons in the episode *Dates*?

906. What kind of vindaloo did Del eat while in Margate on *The Jolly Boys' Outing*?

907. In *Rodney Come Home*, Rodney has a business meeting booked with Mr. Coleman from which company?

908. After Rodney learns that Cassandra is unable to go to Miami in *Miami Twice*, who does Albert first suggest could go in her place?

909. What kind of operation did Del tell Raquel he was going to have in the episode *Modern Men*?

910. In *Time on Our Hands*, what did Albert get mixed up with the gravy granules?

STAGE FRIGHT

Let's see how well you wate after gwappling with these gweat questions!

911. Can you finish this line from Del at the beginning of the episode? "I eat on the move. Mobile phone in one hand, a…"?

912. What offence has Del been charged with, requiring an appearance in court?

913. Who is currently 'doing a very nice line in quality, reject three-piece suites'?

914. While looking for accommodation, the council offer Rodney an LDA. What does he originally suggest an LDA might be?

915. What does an LDA actually turn out to be?

916. What is the last name of Trigger's work-mate Tony, who is also a singer?

917. Where does Trigger say that Tony is performing that evening?

918. What are Rodney's main duties as road manager for the Trotter International Star Agency?

919. Which local villain is now the owner of the Starlight Rooms in Peckham?

920. Who is missing from this list of acts that the local agents offered the Starlight Rooms? 12 strippers, 18 blue comedians, a speciality dog act and…?

CLASS OF 62

A familiar face returns in the fourth episode of series seven.

921. According to Del, Rodney only crawls out of bed when he hears the theme tune to which television programme?

922. Who is the first person to send Del a message on his fax machine?

923. How much did this person pay Del for the fax machine?

924. Which member of the 'Class of 62' organizes a school reunion?

925. Which class were Del, Trigger, Boycie, Denzil and Slater in at school? Class 4A, Class 4B or Class 4C?

926. What time is the school reunion scheduled to start?

927. Which TV prankster does Trigger suggest might have organized the reunion?

928. Who states that "Trigger couldn't organize a prayer in a mosque"?

929. What line of work does Slater say he is in after being released from prison?

930. Who continually has to ask the question "Who's Rachel?"

SPECIALS 9

Time for another round on seasonal specials.

931. What type of disease did Albert say he might get from eating hamburgers in *Rodney Come Home*?

932. According to Trigger in *Time on Our Hands*, who made 'one good film and then you never saw him again'?

933. In *If They Could See Us Now*, Rodney asked Cassandra to dress up as a character from which police series?

934. While making their way over to Holland by boat in *To Hull and Back*, what did Del say Uncle Albert was trying to tune the ship's radio to?

935. True or False – Cassandra's dad Alan couldn't drink on *The Jolly Boys' Outing* because he was on antibiotics?

936. What name does Rodney reveal is an anagram of Frederick Robdal in *The Frog's Legacy*?

937. True or False – In *Fatal Extraction*, it is revealed that Marlene has a tattoo of a heart and dagger on her thigh?

938. Who buys a baby intercom as a present for Damien's christening in *Miami Twice*?

939. In *Time on Our Hands*, what is Del's reply when asked if he is a Naval man?

940. What make of car does Rodney buy for Del in the same episode?

HE AIN'T HEAVY, HE'S MY UNCLE

The fifth episode of the seventh series.

941. Which member of the Trotter family is doing some physical exercises as the episode opens?

942. Which horror film is Del reminded of when he sees Rodney with a hangover?

943. What birthday is Marlene and Boycie's son Tyler celebrating in this episode?

944. Marlene wants to buy Tyler a piano for his birthday. Which rather more mundane musical instrument would Boycie prefer to buy?

945. What make of car does Boycie try to sell to Del to 'suit his image'?

946. What car does Del end up buying from Boycie for £400?

947. When Del sees Albert dressed to impress, complete with his medals, which 80s pop star and keen sailor does he compare him to?

948. Rodney comes back to work for Trotters Independent Traders with which work title?

949. How many muggers does Albert originally say attacked him?

950. What number does this eventually change to?

THREE MEN, A WOMAN AND A BABY

The final episode of series seven sees a new member of the Trotter family enter the world.

951. What is the brand name of the consignment of wigs that Del buys?

952. Whose nephew works for a top West End wig-maker?

953. True or False – Rodney has now become a vegetarian in this episode?

954. Rodney reveals that, with his luck, if he were to be reincarnated he would come back as who?

955. Where do Rodney and Cassandra go for a day out?

956. If Del and Raquel's baby is born a girl, which actress do they want to name her after?

957. What was the name of Trigger's cousin who almost drove his bus over Beachy Head?

958. According to Del, who was in borstal the last time Albert got his leg over?

959. True or False – Del manages to sell a wig to Mike at The Nag's Head?

960. When Raquel is in labour, what makes Del think the baby has a full head of hair?

SPECIALS 10

Time for one last look at some classic seasonal specials.

961. Who got arrested for kicking a football at a police officer in *The Jolly Boys' Outing?*

962. In the episode *Dates*, what did Del guarantee the dating agency that the lucky lady who went on a date with him would get?

963. At Lisa and Andy's wedding in *The Frog's Legacy*, who went around the dance floor pulling all of the men's shirttails out of their trousers?

964. Who did Del buy his fluorescent green silk pyjamas from in *Modern Men?*

965. What is the name of the mafia godfather's son in *Miami Twice?*

966. In the same episode, what is the name of the mafia family's lawyer?

967. How many weeks did the council give Del to clear up Grandad's old allotment in *Mother Nature's Son?* 2, 3 or 4?

968. After becoming a millionaire in *Time on Our Hands*, Del bought Albert a boat. What was the boat called?

969. What did Rodney nickname The Fatty Thumb in *A Royal Flush?*

970. In *Heroes and Villains*, who did Trigger think Del and Rodney were when they were dressed as Batman and Robin?

PUKKA OR PONY?

A true or false round but in true Only Fools style. For each of the following statements, if you think the statement is true then answer Pukka. If you think it is false, your answer is Pony.

971. Grandad's wife was called Alice.

972. Trigger is so-called because he looks like a horse.

973. Del's cousin Stan and his wife Jean live in East London.

974. Both Denzil and Sid used to be bus drivers.

975. While at school, Trigger was Head Boy.

976. Boycie was the goalkeeper for the school football team.

977. Del and Rodney's Great Aunt Rose lives in Southend.

978. Albert and Knock-Knock were at school together.

979. Raquel and Tony rehearse for their performance together at the Jesse Jackson Memorial Hall.

980. Del and Rodney have different blood-groups.

WHO SAID THAT?

Which characters spoke the following lines and which episodes are they from?

981. "I don't want nothing to drink. I'm going back to the hotel to have a fiesta."

982. "What's an ovum?"

983. "Trigger still don't know which end of the dart to throw!"

984. "I lost my dolphin."

985. "It was all blibs and blobs."

986. "What you got? A Wendy House?"

987. "Who's the monk?"

988. "Where's my pork scratchings?"

989. "Here I am trying to clinch a business deal and you've just nicked my client's wig!"

990. "She looks like a Rottweiler in a wig."

FAMOUS LAST WORDS

For which episodes were the following the last lines spoken?

991. "If they started dropping the bomb on us right now, we'd be as safe as houses brother! Safe as houses!"

992. "Trigger's nan was married twice! Oh, no!"

993. "Put that round your Gucci. It'll stop the sole coming off!"

994. "Now don't you start all that blackout nonsense with me Uncle, 'cos it won't wash!"

995. "I don't fancy standing under that water, Del. Not after what I've being doing in it."

996. "I'm gonna stick this right up your jacksy!"

997. "So she was engaged all the time. What a couple of wallies!"

998. "I'm getting married!"

999. "I wouldn't mind betting, this time next week, I'll be in all the papers."

1000. "This time next year we'll be billionaires!"

ANSWERS

Trotter Trivia

1. Nelson Mandela House
2. The Nag's Head
3. New York, Paris, Peckham
4. Three
5. Damien
6. Boycie
7. Uncle Albert
8. Maths and Art
9. Peckham
10. DHV 938D

Del Boy

11. Derek
12. George
13. Bobby Ewing
14. Eels on Wheels
15. Batman
16. Pauline Harris
17. Green Parrot Disease
18. Reg
19. 16
20. Brixton

John Sullivan

21. 1946
22. False – he was born in Balham
23. Charles Dickens
24. Watney's
25. The Two Ronnies
26. True
27. 1983
28. Chas and Dave
29. Heartburn Hotel
30. Four

Big Brother

31. Grandad
32. Because he looks like a horse
33. £200
34. Emperor Burger
35. Harry Belafonte
36. Dougie Sadler
37. Six
38. Draughts
39. Hong Kong
40. He threw them in the river

Debuts

41. Go West Young Man
42. Strained Relations
43. Who's a Pretty Boy?
44. Yuppy Love
45. Dates
46. Who's a Pretty Boy?
47. Big Brother
48. Healthy Competition
49. May the Force Be With You
50. Sleeping Dogs Lie
51. Dates
52. Long Legs of the Law
53. Little Problems
54. Dates
55. Happy Returns

One-Offs

56. Little Problems
57. The Frog's Legacy
58. Stage Fright
59. Who Wants to be a Millionaire
60. Sickness and Wealth

One-Offs cont.

61. The Sky's the Limit
62. Who's a Pretty Boy?
63. Who's a Pretty Boy?
64. Chain Gang
65. The Frog's Legacy
66. Yesterday Never Comes
67. Homesick
68. To Hull and Back
69. The Miracle of Peckham
70. Danger UXD

Trotter by Numbers

71. 714 939
72. £29.48
73. 159
74. 11
75. 3
76. 10
77. 20
78. 3
79. 6
80. 26

Go West Young Man

81. E-Type Jaguar
82. £25
83. £199
84. Vicar
85. Rodney
86. Caribbean Stallion
87. Half a lager
88. Monica
89. Hot Rod
90. Jimmy Connolly

Guest Stars

91. The Frog's Legacy
92. Stage Fright
93. Miami Twice
94. Friday the 14th
95. To Hull and Back
96. Miami Twice
97. A Royal Flush
98. It's Only Rock and Roll
99. If They Could See Us Now
100. Heroes and Villains

Rodney

101. Charlton
102. She was a fan of Charlton Athletic
103. Mickey Pearce
104. Parry Printing
105. £5
106. Mr. Stevens
107. The Indictment
108. Del
109. Frederick Robdal
110. Rodney's mum

Cash and Curry

111. Vauxhall Velox
112. Vimmal Malik
113. Eighteen
114. Odd Job
115. Indian wicket keeper
116. Wealth
117. £4000
118. Low
119. £2000
120. Birmingham, Manchester, Newcastle, Liverpool

The Second Time Around

121. Pork Scratchings
122. Bobby Finch
123. Grandad
124. Baker
125. John Wayne
126. Exchange and Mart
127. Clacton
128. 1947
129. Air Hostess
130. America

Grandad

131. Edward
132. Reg
133. Battle of Rorke's Drift
134. Kilburn
135. False – it was Trigger's nan
136. Horse
137. French Foreign Legion
138. Ada
139. George
140. Thicker Than Water

Little Black Book

141. Del
142. Del
143. Rodney
144. Del
145. Rodney
146. Rodney
147. Del
148. Del
149. Del
150. Rodney

Little Black Book cont.

151. Rodney
152. Del
153. Rodney
154. Rodney
155. Rodney

David Jason – True or False

156. True
157. False
158. False
159. True
160. False
161. True
162. False
163. True
164. False
165. False
166. True
167. True
168. True
169. False
170. True

A Slow Bus to Chingford

171. David Hockney
172. Janice
173. Michaelangelo
174. Nocturnal Security Officer
175. Trotter Watch
176. Tyler Street
177. Attache cases
178. Trotter's Ethnic Tours
179. Abroad
180. Nero

Uncle Albert

181. George and Edward
182. Ada
183. Fred Astaire
184. Rum
185. True
186. Boomerang Trotter
187. USS Pittsburgh
188. Gladstone
189. Stan and Jean
190. Elsie Partridge

Nicholas Lyndhurst

191. 1961
192. True
193. Going Straight
194. Adam
195. Janet Dibley
196. Patrick Troughton
197. The Piglet Files
198. Laurence Marks and Maurice Gran
199. Six
200. Freddy Robdal

The Russians are Coming

201. Rodney
202. Three
203. Air Raid Shelter
204. Eric
205. "…Mine is but to sell and buy."
206. Inch War
207. His moustache
208. Passchendaele
209. Audie Murphy
210. Rock Hudson

Christmas Crackers

211. 1981
212. False – Neither of them appear
213. Mickey Pearce
214. Bag of giblets
215. Brenda and Terry
216. Custard
217. The Circus
218. Monte Carlo Club
219. Earl
220. Crufts

Guest Stars 2

221. The Jolly Boys' Outing
222. Little Problems
223. The Longest Night
224. Mother Nature's Son
225. Little Problems
226. The Unlucky Winner Is
227. Time on Our Hands
228. Modern Men
229. The Miracle of Peckham
230. Dates

Trigger

231. Colin Ball
232. Dave
233. False – he has a sister
234. Eighteen
235. Julie Christie
236. Marilyn
237. Councillor Murray
238. Fourteen
239. A pork pie
240. Lisa

The Long Legs of the Law

241. His false teeth
242. Tommy Razzle
243. The Exterminator
244. Walking on the Moon
245. Grandad
246. Cashews
247. 24 hours
248. Walworth Road
249. Plimsoles
250. After-shave

Ashes to Ashes

251. Sacha Distel
252. Alice
253. Linda's
254. His father
255. True
256. Ireland
257. Fifteen
258. Peckham Bowling Club
259. St. Catherine's Dock
260. Twice

A Losing Streak

261. Double-headed coin
262. None
263. £150
264. Kempton Park
265. £4.37
266. Paul Daniels
267. £500
268. His car
269. Four
270. Ace

Boycie

271. King's Avenue
272. Aubrey
273. Cornwall
274. Bronco
275. Duke
276. The Masons
277. Satellite Dish
278. False – Earl is the name of their Rottweiler
279. Shropshire
280. Elgin Sparrowhawk

No Greater Love

281. Camel hair coat
282. Mackay
283. East London
284. Parkhurst
285. Tommy Mackay
286. Starsky and Hutch
287. True
288. Monkey Harris
289. Rodney
290. Zoe

Lennard Pearce

291. 1915
292. True
293. Adolf Hitler
294. True
295. David Jason
296. Coronation Street
297. Hammer
298. False
299. 23
300. 1984

Hooky Street

301. As One Door Closes
302. Fatal Extraction
303. Heroes and Villains
304. Chance of a Lunchtime
305. Danger UXD
306. A Losing Streak
307. Miami Twice
308. Three Men, A Woman and a Baby
309. Dates
310. The Frog's Legacy

The Yellow Peril

311. The Golden Lotus
312. Mr. Chin
313. £150
314. Blue
315. Clapham Junction
316. Monkey Harris
317. Painting signs in tunnels
318. London
319. Stockholm
320. Heathrow

It Never Rains

321. Alex
322. 80%
323. Benidorm
324. Luton
325. Plenty of pepper
326. Jackie
327. 1936
328. Peckham Rye
329. Spanish Civil War
330. Jay-walking

Buster Merryfield

331. 1920
332. Harry
333. True
334. Banking
335. True
336. Lennard Pearce
337. 1985
338. 37
339. To Hull and Back
340. 1999

Denzil

341. Corrine
342. Five
343. Carl
344. 13
345. Sylvester
346. Jam sponge
347. £2000
348. Ear infection
349. Transworld Express
350. Peckham Courier Service

A Touch of Glass

351. How Much is that Doggie in the Window?
352. Lewisham
353. Wallace
354. Canaletto
355. Cambridge
356. 17th-century
357. £1200
358. £350
359. The plague
360. Buckingham Palace

Diamonds are for Heather

361. Enrico
362. Old Shep
363. Brixton
364. Brian
365. Mayfair and Penthouse
366. False – Darren is her son.
367. Rodney
368. Uncle Ben's
369. Abdul
370. Father Christmas

John Challis

371. 1942
372. Open All Hours
373. True
374. Bristol
375. Coronation Street
376. Tom Baker
377. True
378. 33
379. Howards' Way
380. True

Homesick

381. Basil or Baz
382. Miss Mackenzie
383. Haddock Pie
384. Dr. Becker
385. The Archers
386. Medical profession
387. Crossroads
388. Oranges
389. Cigarette case
390. Rorke's Drift

Roger Lloyd Pack

391. 1944
392. Charles Lloyd Pack
393. True
394. Health and Efficiency
395. Two Point Four Children
396. Owen Newitt
397. Harry Potter and the Goblet of Fire
398. Clive Swift
399. 39
400. False

Healthy Competition

401. Prince William
402. Burma
403. Mickey Pearce
404. Lot 36 – Cut-glass goblets
405. Lot 37
406. Alfie Flowers
407. Benidorm
408. £200
409. £165
410. Parks Department

Mike

411. Kenneth Macdonald
412. Fisher
413. 18
414. On a cruise ship
415. Albert
416. Electric paint stripper
417. Eddie Chambers
418. The Mardi Gras
419. Embezzling money from the brewery
420. Sid

Friday the 14th

421. Boycie's
422. Mario's
423. Grandad
424. Monopoly
425. Chief Robson
426. "A geezer what dresses up in his mother's clothes."
427. Tom Witton
428. Barratts
429. Snooker
430. £10

Yesterday Never Comes

431. Queen Anne
432. £145
433. Davenport
434. Chelsea
435. Queen Elizabeth II
436. The Chinese Detective
437. A Citroen manual
438. Penthouse
439. Huddlestone's
440. Joshua Blythe

Hooky Street 2

441. The Jolly Boys' Outing
442. Danger UXD
443. Big Brother
444. It Never Rains
445. Mother Nature's Son
446. As One Door Closes
447. The Frog's Legacy
448. Danger UXD
449. Heroes and Villains
450. Fatal Extraction

Mickey Pearce

451. Patrick Murray
452. 1983
453. Monica
454. Financial Director
455. The Bay City Rollers
456. The World of Leather
457. Boots
458. Jevon
459. Ian Beale
460. 19

May the Force be with You

461. Detective Inspector
462. Boycie
463. Rodney
464. The Dukes of Hazzard
465. "…an entire lawn!"
466. Tyres
467. Terry Hoskins
468. £50
469. Long John Silver
470. Del

Wanted

471. Blossom
472. A doctor
473. The Peckham Pouncer
474. Grandad
475. Charing Cross, Soho, Leicester Square
476. Under his bed
477. Johnny Cash, Live at San Quentin
478. Cat
479. He forgot the tin opener
480. The kebab house

During the War

481. The Russian convoys
482. Captain Kenworthy
483. Trotter's Trembler
484. Tubby Fox
485. HMS Peerless
486. Boiler maintenance man
487. Isle of Wight
488. Helga
489. Lion
490. Sid

Cassandra

491. Gwyneth Strong
492. Parry
493. Louise
494. Alan and Pamela
495. Blackheath
496. Emma
497. A bank
498. Adult Education Centre
499. Rimini
500. 21

Who's a Pretty Boy?

501. O'Shaughnessy
502. Battleship grey
503. It was genuine camel hair
504. Dublin
505. Papering over a serving hatch
506. £100
507. The Magna Carta
508. Ginger Ted
509. Italian Louis
510. £45

Thicker than Water

511. Lassie
512. 1965
513. Cubic Foot
514. Newcastle
515. Hereditary blood disorder
516. AB
517. Trumpet
518. Adam Faith
519. The zoo
520. Porter

Raquel

521. Tessa Peake-Jones
522. Rachel Turner
523. Technomatch Friendship and Matrimonial Agency
524. Hilton Hotel, Park Lane
525. Antiques
526. Doctor Who
527. Double Cream
528. My Fair Lady
529. The Great Ramondo
530. Slow Boat to China

Marlene

531. Sue Holderness
532. Lane
533. Dora
534. False – it is her brother
535. Bookmakers
536. True
537. Mark
538. Twenty
539. Breast enlargement
540. Series 4

Happy Returns

541. Newsagents
542. Jason
543. Albie Littlewood
544. Trilby
545. Zimbabwe House
546. 19 years
547. Duran Duran
548. Stealing some watches
549. 7 years
550. False

Strained Relations

551. Brother
552. Trigger
553. Cigarette machine
554. George
555. Insurance
556. £86
557. Sausage and Mash
558. Audrey
559. St Catherine's Dock
560. £100

Specials

561. Imogen
562. Duke of Maylebury
563. Handsome Sansom
564. Trigger's
565. Stephen
566. Harry
567. Trigger
568. Brighton
569. Michelle
570. Gerbil

Births, Weddings and Anniversaries

571. True
572. Joanne and Stephen
573. Hampshire
574. Trigger
575. Thirteen
576. £2000
577. Rodney and Cassandra
578. Mickey Pearce
579. Her mother
580. Car stereo

Hole in One

581. Suntan lotion
582. £500
583. Deep-fat fryer
584. Rodney
585. A summons
586. Solly Attwell
587. £2000
588. Ten
589. The Krypton Factor
590. The Ferret

It's Only Rock and Roll

591. Four
592. Drums
593. Mental Mickey Maguire
594. Frankie Goes to Hollywood
595. Viv Richards
596. The Dublin Bay Stormers
597. Liam
598. £300
599. A Bunch of Wallies
600. Boys Will be Boys

Slater

601. Jim Broadbent
602. Roy
603. Ruby
604. 4 years
605. Parkhurst
606. Stamps
607. Trigger
608. Del
609. 18
610. Bulldog

Trotter Music

611. Eric Clapton
612. Bros
613. Hey There, You With the Stars in Your Eyes
614. Tubular Bells by Mike Oldfield
615. Feargal Sharkey
616. Mike Read
617. One Voice
618. Help
619. Crying
620. Desert Inn, Las Vegas

Sleeping Dogs Lie

621. £600
622. £60
623. Seychelles
624. Chum
625. Mr. Collis
626. "...pork!"
627. Del
628. Frankenstein
629. Roast pork
630. Albert's sleeping pills

Watching the Girls Go By

631. £2.50
632. Uncle Albert
633. Big Brenda
634. "…Bertie Bassett."
635. Paddy the Greek
636. In his Wranglers
637. Right
638. Yvonne or Vonny
639. She is a stripper
640. 50p

As One Door Closes

641. Brendan O'Shaughnessy
642. Louvre
643. Teddy Cummings
644. On yer bike!
645. Jamaican Swallowtail
646. £3000
647. False – it was Greenwich Park
648. True
649. 165
650. Rodney

Specials 2

651. The Norland
652. The Jolly Boys' Outing
653. Trigger
654. Sotheby's
655. June Snell
656. Gold Rush
657. Mel Gibson
658. Del
659. Blue
660. Ochetti

Del's Foreign Lingo

661. Ajax
662. Vorsprung durch Technik
663. French
664. "…Bonjour!"
665. Dates
666. USA
667. "Fromage Frais!"
668. The Frog's Legacy
669. Furniture store
670. The Jolly Boys' Outing

From Prussia with Love

671. 1986
672. Swedish
673. Albert
674. "Vot ees your nem?"
675. One year
676. English and French
677. Blake Carrington
678. Spencer Wainwright
679. Boycie and Marlene
680. West Indies

The Miracle of Peckham

681. Kippers
682. Joan Collins
683. Helen of Croydon
684. Biffo
685. £20
686. £185,000
687. St Mary's
688. Samantha Fox
689. Boycie buying a round
690. NBC

The Nag's Head

691. Joycie
692. True
693. £1
694. Elsie Partridge
695. £2.50
696. Metropolitan Water Board
697. Comedian
698. Albert
699. 16
700. Pies

The Longest Night

701. Topbuy Superstores
702. Sheila
703. £1000
704. Tom Clarke
705. Mr. Peterson
706. Gilby
707. 6pm
708. The Shadow
709. Epidemics
710. When he wipes the cobwebs off his head

Specials 3

711. 98
712. A chauffeur
713. The Beatles manager
714. Undertakers
715. Hussein
716. Paris
717. Virgin
718. Carmen
719. Del
720. Russell Crowe

Tea for Three

721. Aunt Ada
722. Liberace
723. Miss 999
724. 25
725. Roy Orbison
726. Dream Topping
727. Cheese
728. False – it was Del
729. 46th
730. Mike and Trigger

Video Nasty

731. Some soldiers
732. Boycie
734. Mr. Stevens
735. Rodney Trotter wristwatch
736. Mickey Pearce
737. There's a Rhino Loose in the City
738. Marlene
739. Spanish Omelette
740. A and T

Who Wants to be a Millionaire?

741. £10
742. Sydney
743. $500,000
744. True
745. Nervous disorder
746. 1967
747. £200
748. Dillingers
749. Car cleaner
750. The men spit further

Specials 4

751. Thirty
752. Time on Our Hands
753. Denzil
754. Cassandra
755. Albert
756. Villa Bella
757. Mrs. Creswell
758. Monkey Harris
759. £145,000
760. Patterson

Yuppy Love

761. 1989
762. 2 years
763. Gordon Gekko
764. Grandad
765. Two
766. Mountbatten Estate
767. Mickey Pearce
768. Blackheath
769. £20
770. Tower of London

Danger UXD

771. Formosa
772. Advanced Electronics Research and Development Centre
773. Ronnie Nelson
774. 50
775. A slice of bread
776. Deptford
777. 50
778. Dirty Barry
779. Boycie
780. Propane

Specials 5

781. A bic
782. J. Hawker Haulage
783. Limpy Lionel
784. Eastbourne
785. Ivor Hardy
786. Ronnie Nelson
787. £175
788. 1965
789. Jelly Kelly
790. Lennie Norris

Around Peckham

791. Arnold Road
792. Tanya
793. Otto
794. The Coach and Horses
795. High Street
796. True
797. The Legion
798. Neyere Estate
799. Peckham Echo
800. The Light of Nepal

Chain Gang

801. The One Eleven Club
802. Alan Parry
803. Pat
804. False – they are called Gary and Stephen
805. 250
806. £12500
807. Mike
808. Boycie
809. Albert
810. St Stephen's Hospital

The Unlucky Winner Is

811. Marble Arch at Dawn
812. Arc de Triomphe
813. Marie Whittaker
814. Elsie Partridge
815. Mega Flakes
816. Mallorca
817. The Groovy Gang
818. 2nd
819. Alan Perkins
820. One million pesetas

Specials 6

821. Mickey Pearce
822. Denzil
823. Nature's Way
824. Honey, I Shrunk the Kids
825. Zippy and Bungle
826. Two
827. Trigger
828. Because he was a Navy frogman
829. Australia
830. 6.2 million pounds

Motor Madness

831. Go West Young Man
832. Go West Young Man
833. Cash and Curry
834. He Ain't Heavy, He's My Uncle
835. Slow Bus to Chingford
836. Cash and Curry
837. Chain Gang
838. The Frog's Legacy
839. Time on Our Hands
840. Ashes to Ashes

Sickness and Wealth

841. £20
842. £10
843. Positive Mental Attitude
844. Bathroom
845. Sixties
846. Battersea Dogs Home
847. £20
848. Dr. Shaheed
849. New Delhi
850. Irritable Bowel Syndrome

Little Problems

851. £6000
852. 100
853. £40
854. Dartford
855. £150
856. The Planet of the Apes
857. £2000
858. Denzil
859. Pie and Mash shop
860. True

Specials 7

861. Spa Water and Natural Springs Committee
862. Rodney
863. Percy's Luxury Tours
864. Mickey
865. Fiji
866. Albert's
867. Lurch
868. Piranha
869. Apple juice
870. Epping Forest

The Sky's the Limit

871. Financial Times and Exchange and Mart
872. A Lada
873. 81
874. Belly ache
875. £400
876. Kylie
877. Linda
878. Leroy
879. £500
880. 18 months

Chance of a Lunchtime

881. As You Like It
882. Aida
883. 36
884. £13
885. Andrew Ridgeley
886. He will play Mexico Forever on the front door
887. Spain
888. Del and Rodney's mum Joan
889. Jules
890. He prefers Castella

Behind the Scenes

891. Bobby Bragg
892. True
893. True
894. Martin Shardlow
895. Chas and Dave
896. Felix Bowness
897. Gareth Gwenlan
898. True
899. Mandie Fletcher and Susan Belbin
900. False

Specials 8

901. Gold identity bracelets
902. 45p
903. A spoonful of rum to keep it moist
904. Trigger
905. Boycie
906. Lobster
907. Classic Curtains
908. Mickey Pearce
909. Vasectomy
910. Maxwell House coffee

Stage Fright

911. "...Pot Noodle in the other."
912. Fly pitching
913. Young Towser
914. Luxury Detached Abode
915. Low Demand Accommodation
916. Angelino
917. Down by the Riverside club
918. Sweep up and make the tea
919. Eugene McCarthy
920. Lionel Blair

Class of 62

921. Home and Away
922. Mike
923. £45
924. Slater
925. 4C
926. 7:30pm
927. Jeremy Beadle
928. Boycie
929. Undertakers
930. Albert

Specials 9

931. Mad Cow Disease
932. Gandhi
933. The Bill
934. The Kid Jensen Show
935. False – it was Denzil
936. Alfred Broderick
937. True
938. Marlene
939. "I'm more of a leg man myself."
940. Rolls Royce

He Ain't Heavy, He's My Uncle

941. Albert
942. A Nightmare on Elm Street
943. 2nd
944. Mouth organ
945. Skoda
946. Capri Ghia
947. Simon Le Bon
948. Director of Commercial Development
949. Four
950. Six

Three Men, a Woman and a Baby

951. Crowning Glory
952. Mustapha's
953. True
954. Himself
955. Hampton Court
956. Sigourney Weaver
957. Cyril
958. Nelson Mandela
959. False – he sold one to Trigger
960. The midwife's wig falls off onto the bed

Specials 10

961. Rodney
962. A steak meal
963. Marlene
964. Monkey Harris
965. Rico
966. Salvatore
967. Two weeks
968. Princess Khadija
969. Sid's Café
970. Lone Ranger and Tonto

Pukka or Pony

971. False
972. True
973. False
974. True
975. True
976. False
977. False
978. True
979. True
980. False

Who Said That?

981. Grandad in *It Never Rains*
982. Albert in *Heroes and Villains*
983. Mike in *Mother Nature's Son*
984. Trigger in *The Jolly Boys' Outing*
985. Albert in *Dates*
986. Grandad in *Healthy Competition*
987. Dirty Barry in *Danger UXD*
988. Rodney in *The Second Time Around*
989. Boycie in *Who Wants to be a Millionaire?*
990. Del in *Rodney Come Home*

Famous Last Words

991. The Russians are Coming
992. Ashes to Ashes
993. Healthy Competition
994. Hole in One
995. Wanted
996. It's Only Rock and Roll
997. Tea for Three
998. Sickness and Wealth
999. Mother Nature's Son
1000. Time on Our Hands

Printed by Amazon Italia Logistica S.r.l.
Torrazza Piemonte (TO), Italy